Seaton, Axmouth, Colyton, Colyford, Beer & Branscombe Companion

by Sheila Bird

First published 1986
Reprinted 1988 & 2001

ISBN 0-9512236-2-3

Bird of Freedom,
The Shrubbery,
17, Grovehill Drive,
Falmouth,
Cornwall TR11 3HS
01326 211323

ACKNOWLEDGEMENTS

I should like to thank Mr. Philip Noakes for contributing the Wildlife and Conservation section on the Axe Valley, and my brother, Dr. Eric Bird for advising on the scientific and geological aspects.

* * * * *

Maps and illustrations are by the author.

ABOUT THE AUTHOR

Sheila Bird, a former teacher is now a full time writer and journalist contributing to a variety of national and local newspapers and magazines. She is a member of The West Country Writers' Association and The Society of Authors.

Her other books include:

Bygone Falmouth.
Bygone Truro.
Bygone Penzance & Newlyn.
County Companions Dorset.
The Book of Somerset Villages.
The Book of Cornish Villages.
Lyme Regis, Uplyme & Charmouth Companion.
Sidmouth, Budleigh Salterton & District Companion.
Exmouth, The Exe Estuary & Dawlish Companion.

* * * *

Phoenician Trader

SEATON

Introduction

The popular East Devon resort of Seaton enjoys an enviable situation on the western side of the Axe estuary and along the south facing shores of Seaton Bay, incorporated in Lyme Bay. Protected from landward by the characteristic rolling dark green hills flanking the beautiful Axe Valley, and dominated by the contrasting twin portals of Haven Cliff to the east and White Cliff to the west the resort has the advantages of an open, mile long section of sand and shingle beach.

Seaton is a place which caters for every taste. For those who enjoy the outdoor life there are opportunities for boating, angling, deep sea fishing, sunbathing, swimming, walking and a variety of sports, and there is the unique opportunity of taking a tram ride along the estuary of the Axe and up to Colyton. The resort also offers a range of indoor attractions. The area is of particular interest for geologists, archaeologists, ornithologists and anyone interested in natural history.

SEATON'S HEALTHY CLIMATE

Sheltered by hills and headlands and with a south facing coastal situation, Seaton is a suntrap with a year round, equable climate which gives rise to interesting and luxuriant plant life.

The place has inherited the reputation for its mild and healthy climate. A guidebook published at the beginning of the century described it as an ideal resting spot for retired Indian Army officers and civil servants, and with its rejuvenating, health-giving qualities, particularly advocated it for those who had ruined their health in the course of making their fortunes in festering foreign climes! Back in 1880 a physician prescribed it as 'a halfway house for the weary pilgrim on his way back from the gates of Death to the Elysium of Good Health', while in 1907, medics proclaimed it, 'Perhaps the most bracing place on the Devonshire South Coast.'

Seaton Beach

THE BEACH

The clear, intense light heightens the subtle blend of contrasting colours of the cliffs and the shoreline. The cliffs to the east and to the west are predisposed to rapid erosion and sudden subsidence because of the nature of the geological strata. Beautiful stones including garnets, beryls and jaspers can be found along the shingle beach, which is constantly being swept by wave action to form a ridge blocking the entrance to the haven.

There is an Esplanade extending from the pebble ridge to the east below the imposing Haven Cliff to the towering, chalk, ivy clad White Cliff to the west. In former times there was a coalyard near the Esplanade Hotel, and the old barges were drawn up on the beach to enable their cargoes to be loaded and unloaded onto waiting horse-drawn carts. At the beginning of this century the Council provided a wide canvas screen for the convenience of visitors wishing to take early morning dips in the sea.

From the top of Haven Cliff and White Cliff there are magnificent, panoramic views from Portland to Start Point and inland up the beautiful, green and pastoral Axe Valley.

SEATON ..... By any other name

Prior to the Norman Conquest, the old name for Seaton had been 'Aut Fleote'.

THE PHOENICIAN CONNECTION

There is evidence that the early Phoenician traders, who were the first to visit England had connections with the Dorset coast, and it is thought likely that they might have sailed up the haven in the days when the estuary was wide and navigable and on the early trading routes. Phoenician coins discovered in Dorset were exhibited by The Society of Antiquaries in 1832.

SEATON DOWN

The grassed over earthworks on Seaton Down, are thought to have been a medieval animal-pound. There were frequent confrontations between the Dumnonii tribe of Devonshire and the Durotriges, who occupied both sides of the Axe Valley. These were the most powerful of the tribes frequenting the South West, each possessing its own language, laws and customs. The area was also subject to frequent invasions by sea.

THE ROMAN CONNECTION

The haven which had been navigable up to Musbury and beyond was an established port before the arrival of the Romans. They developed it into one of the most important of the commercial ports along the South Coast and improved land communications. Iron from the Mendips and wool from the Cotswolds was exported from the port which many people believe to have been the very important port of Moridunum at the time of Vespasian.

Hembury Fort near Honiton and Peak Hill near Sidmouth are other contenders for this piece of historical recognition.

Uncertainty to the claim of Seaton being the genuine Moridunum there may well be, but one former Lord of the Manor, obviously subscribing to the theory that if you press a point forcibly enough for long enough, the notion gains credibility arranged for the seaward face of the Esplanade to bear the word MORIDUNUM to be written large and clear for all to see.

The area around Seaton has been rich in Roman finds. There were two Roman villas in Seaton, one at Membury and another at Holcombe, near Uplyme. A mound in the centre of the Seaton Esplanade was built to mount a fort. In 1544 Henry VIII called in on his return from Calais to see 'my new (wooden) fort'.

ROMAN THOROUGHFARES

Two important Roman military thoroughfares run through the Axe Valley; the Icknield Way and the Fosse Way. The Fosse Way, making its straight course from Lincoln, Cirencester, Bath and Exeter linked with the southern branch incorporating Axminster and running down to the busy port at Axmouth Haven.

Viking Warrior

Roman Merchant Ship

Roman Soldier

5

THE ADRIATIC CONNECTION

In the 19th century a memorial stone was discovered at Salona on the Adriatic coast, dedicated to 'A noble lady member of the community of the Dumnonii', who was born in A.D. 395 and died in 425. This must refer to a female member of the local tribe who married into the upper levels of the Roman hierarchy and returned with her family to her husband's homeland; quite an undertaking in those early days.

LOST IN ANTIQUITY

It is known that the importance of the haven had started to diminish before the 15th century, as a result of the movement of the shingle bar which blockaded the harbour entrance. Axmouth's loss resulted in ships being diverted to neighbouring Lyme Regis which then began to thrive as a trading port. The mud of the haven must still bear many clues and ancient keels, nails, chains, anchors and decaying timber skeletons of old vessels have been discovered. An anchor was excavated way upstream at Axminster.

The area marked on old maps as 'Merchant's Road', now a section of marsh land east of Seaton Church is likely to have been the place where ships anciently loaded and discharged their cargoes. Harepath Road, derived from the Anglo-Saxon word 'Herr' meaning a warrior, would indicate a 'track of the warriors' — or a military way.

VULNERABLE TO ATTACK

There were frequent attacks and invasions all along the south coast of England, and Seaton, at the mouth of the Axe was particularly inviting to invaders. In 937, following plunderous exploits in Scotland and the north east, the warring Danes, led by Anlaf turned their attentions to the south coast. It is thought that they landed at Seaton without attracting much attention and proceeded to set up camp on Hanna Hill where they could maintain surveillance of the surrounding countryside and be within sight of their anchored fleet. The terrified local people lit beacons on the hillsides, which was the traditional warning of danger, and then fled. In those days when kings took to the battlefields and personally led their troops, the Saxon King Athelstan and other leaders set up camps around the valley. Meanwhile Anlaf, who wanted to glean information on enemy strategy hit upon the idea of disguising himself as a strolling minstrel to gain access to the Saxon camp. He was audacious enough to get himself to the royal tent, and apparently pleased King Athelstan so much with his songs and quips that he was given a present of money for his efforts. The giving and receiving of 'tips' being an admission of higher and lower status, the Dane unwillingly took it, but promptly buried it as soon as he thought he was out of sight. This action was witnessed by a soldier who had formerly been under his command.

THE BATTLE OF BRUNENBURGH

During the ensuing battle the Axe Valley air was rent with shouts and cries of agony and victory and it was reported that the river ran red with the blood. Anlaf's surviving soldiers fled from the body strewn battle field, hurriedly rejoined their ships and retreated to Ireland.

THE FATES AND FORTUNES OF SEATON

In 1005 King Aethelred granted Seaton and some adjoining land to a Thegn called Eadsig. On his death it passed to the Priory of Horton, in East Dorset and thence to the Priory of Sherborne in 1122. At the time of the Dissolution it went to Catherine Parr and to John Frye three years later. It passed on to the Willoughby family and to the Trevelyans in 1656.

SEATON GRANTED A WEEKLY MARKET AND A YEARLY FAIR

Edward I granted Seaton a weekly market and a yearly fair 'on the eve, the day, and the morrow of St Gregory the Martyr, with all liberties and free customs appertaining to such a market and fair, unless that market and fair be injurious to neighbouring markets and fairs.' The market disappeared but the pleasure fair continued to be held half yearly on Whit Tuesday with amusements, games and various entertaining diversions while boating trips operated from the beach.

THE CALAIS CONNECTION

In 1347 Seaton sent 2 ships and 25 men for the Siege of Calais. Neighbouring Lyme provided 4 ships and 62 men, while Portsmouth sent 5 ships and 96 men.

THE DECLINE OF THE HAVEN

The fallen glory of the haven at the time of the Middle Ages was made clear by the historian Leland who wrote in 1538: 'The river Axe is dryven to the est point of the haven and ther, at a very smaul gut, goith into the se.'

The towering Haven Cliff at the silted up mouth of the Axe

ATTEMPTS TO RESTORE THE HAVEN

Various attempts were made to clear the haven throughout the ages, but to little avail. In 1450 Bishop Lacy made an appeal to his flock to get busy on clearing the blocked haven by appealing to their sense of religious duty. 'Forty days' indulgence would be granted to true penitents'.

Henry VIII and Queen Elizabeth also attempted to raise money by subscription for the repair of the haven. In the early 17th century the Erle family of Bindon spent a great deal of time and money trying to improve the situation of the silted up harbour and in the 19th century local farmers sent their workers along to dig it out. Unfortunately a storm and flood destroyed all their hard work and the project was abandoned.

More recently Mr. Hallett of Stedcombe Manor spent large sums of money on an excavation project, but his efforts were not backed up by the government as many people felt they ought to have been. Thus the pier became increasingly battered and the harbour continued to deteriorate.

THE LEGEND OF THE STONE SEA WALL

The explanation of the origin of the long pier consisting of great rocks piled together which jutted out near the mouth of the haven was that many years ago, a poor sailor called Courd was approached by a Greek in the Mediterranean and told of a great treasure buried at the top of 'Hogsdon Hill.' The informative stranger explained that his ancestors had let him in on the little secret. Returning to these shores the sailor eagerly grabbed a spade and got digging and as luck would have it he came upon a golden hoarde. (It is rumoured that a number of 'hopefuls' carried out further enthusiastic digging, but failed to strike it rich). However, the sailor was so grateful for his newly acquired wealth that he built the wall in an effort to restore the beach, at his own expense.

TITHES OF FISH

Occupational 'perks' for 'men of the cloth' may have been many and varied. At Seaton and Beer the vicars were entitled to a percentage share of flat fish, such as turbot, sole and plaice which were caught in a 'tucking net', as well as a share of 'threading fish', caught with a hook and line, such as whiting. Records indicate that the owners of boats and nets kept exaggerated accounts of their deductable expenses so that the vicars' 'net' profits were as minimal as possible. These old records also reveal that some of the local fishermen went to the Newfoundland fisheries.

COASTAL FORTIFICATIONS

In 1627 the Deputy Lieutenants of Devon made a formal request for more guns and better military coastal defences pointing out that Seaton needed to be able to readily protect itself from seaward attack by pirates and other enemies. They wrote a report stating: 'In former times, when there has been hostility between France and England, the bay before Seaton and Sidmouth, being very open, had been fortified with ordnance which is now unserviceable.' The ordnance referred to was probably given to the county of Devon by Henry VIII.

The concrete Axmouth Bridge

AN EMERGING RESORT

Before the arrival of the railway Seaton had been a quiet village consisting mainly of cob walled, thatched cottages, and a small population gleaning a livelihood from fishing, farming and the lessening sea borne trade. At a time when seaside places were becoming fashionable, and seawater and bathing were thought to be beneficial to health, the coming of the railway effectively put Seaton on the map as a rising resort. Thus the rather quiet and isolated village sprouted lodging houses, hotels and shops and many of the old cottages were swept away as Seaton began to emerge as a modern watering place. Possibly they were a little over enthusiastic in their desire to be up-to-date, for very few of the older buildings remain in Seaton. Today, just a few of the original old cottages remain, dotted around the town amongst the other buildings.

THE VANISHED 'BARROW', PHAROS AND CUSTOM HOUSE

On the seafront a mound known as the 'Barrow' was emplaced to assist coastal defences at a cost of £24. On this stood the square old lighthouse or 'pharos' which was 16 feet high, and served as a navigational aid to shipping. Beside it were 2 mounted guns. The old Custom House at the mouth of the Axe which had served the tall masted ships was demolished in 1915.

HONEY DITCHES

The attractive name of 'Honey Ditches' or 'Hanna Ditches' is thought to be a corruption of 'Anlaf' ditches, based on the supposition that the Battle of Brununburgh in 957 between King Athelstan and the invading Danes under the command of Anlaf was fought in this valley. Modern researchers regard the name as Medieval, meaning 'muddy'.

13

LOVERS' LANE

In former times Marlpit Lane was generally acknowledged as 'Lovers' Lane'.

THE PEBBLES ON THE BEACH

Over the years thousands of tons of pebbles have been removed from the beach, a practice which has been carried on along sections of this coastline, which many acknowledge to have contributed sharply to the erosion problem. After the last war a pebble company was formed and some local people found employment as pebble graders. In the days of 'What's My Line?', a Seaton pebble picker, who specialised in picking beryl, jasper and garnet, beat the 'Whats My Line' panel. When the Rural District Council took over, the extraction of pebbles from the beach was stopped.

THE SEATON TRAMWAY

Having been deprived of their rail link in 1966, the folk of Seaton were fortunate that Modern Electric Tramways Limited which had been operating at Eastbourne was able to take over the line to operate a service between Seaton and Colyton. The attractive trams, run by the company now known as Seaton Tramway are particularly appreciated by holidaymakers, tram enthusiasts, bird watchers, people interested in local history and residents who use them as regular transport. The trams are available for chartering by groups. (Seaton 21702)

SEATON TODAY

In common with many other places along the South Coast Seaton has grown in recent years and it is much favoured by people moving from other areas, retirement folk, tram enthusiasts and the holidaymakers who are attracted by its lovely setting, good facilities, friendly people and the attractive way of life in East Devon.

* * * * *

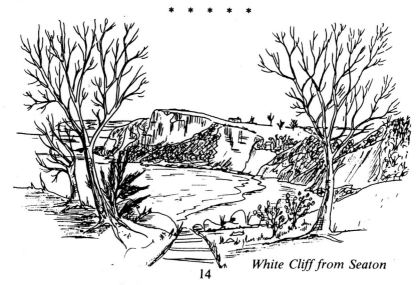

White Cliff from Seaton

14

THE DECLINE OF THE ESTUARY
OF THE AXE

What a magnificent sight the estuary of the Axe must have made in the great days of sail when it was wider and navigable by early trading ships. Following the blocking of the harbour mouth, probably before the Middle Ages the estuary has become more and more restricted. In 1911 Francis Bickley wrote: 'Not so many generations ago, long since Leland's time, tall ships might ride at anchor where the Axe merges with the sea. But the river, which made the harbour, has been its destruction; that, and the busy modern spirit of progress, which has no use for the little town, the little port, but prefers to concentrate its energies in a few great cities, dirty and impersonal. For a long time the men of Seaton and Axmouth fought hard against the wasting of the sea and the silting of the river. But, getting no encouragement, they at last desisted.'

In 1875 it had been recorded that, 'prior to the erection of the pier, about 1803, the river did not regularly flow into the sea, but remained kept back like a three quarter tide and overflowed a portion of the Marsh .... Even at high tides the stream had a flow at its mouth of not more than four or five feet, and at other times the water percolated through the shingle, as the Char does at Charmouth.'

So what is the scientific explanation for this?

THE ESTUARY OF THE AXE

By the end of the Ice Age, the Axe Valley had been cut down below the present sea level and the river flowed out across the floor of the English Channel. At that time the sea level was lower. The sea level has risen and about 5,000 or 6,000 years ago the Axe Estuary would have been a long inlet of the sea at least as far as Colyford, probably further. Then the sea level rise stopped and the river which was washing down sand, silt and clay from the Axe Valley started to fill in that inlet.

At the same time the shingle beach at Seaton built up and grew eastwards to constrict and deflect the outlet of the estuary. This made the water even more sheltered. Waves would no longer run up the inlet, so it became a place of quiet, muddy sedimentation.

As the mud built up from the head of the inlet and along its sides it came up above mid tide level and was then colonised by salt marsh, followed by reed swamp. So the muddy estuary we now see is a much shrunken remnant of the much bigger inlet that existed 6,000 years ago. In fact it was bigger in Roman times, 2,000 years ago, when Fosse Way ended at Axmouth and the Romans were able to use it as a port.

Since Roman times there has probably been a rise of the sea level, due to the sinking of the land along the south coast, and although this probably only amounts to 1 or 2 metres it may mean that the site of the Roman harbour is at a lower level, buried by shingle or mud and submerged by the sea.

In the last 40 years Spartina grass has been introduced and this has built up in front of the earlier salt marshes, especially down the western side, trapping mud along the estuary sides.

What is happening now is that slowly the situation is continuing and perhaps in a century or so it will all be marshes, with the Axe just a tidal creek winding through to the sea like the nearby Otter is now. The Axe is still an open estuary.

* * * * *

THE IMPORTANCE OF THE ESTUARY
AS A HABITAT FOR WILDLIFE

As Britain's wetlands steadily diminish, the estuary of the Axe with its marshes, reedbeds and areas of wet meadowland provides an important and varied habitat for a range of wildlife, particularly birds. Much is being done by the Axe Vale & District Conservation Society to safeguard the future of this important area, and their Borrow Pit project has been effective in attracting a wide variety of birds. Reedbeds along the south coast provide a vital source of food and shelter for outward and returning migrant birds.

The stunningly beautiful sight of the sunset reflected in the waters of the Axe as evening flocks of birds are silhouetted against the ever changing, darkening sky is an unforgettable experience.

* * * * *

THE ESTUARY AND MARSHES

The estuary and marshes now cover a fairly small area extending about 2½ miles northwards from the river mouth at Haven Cliffs to the present limit of tidal water near Axe Bridge at Colyford. At high tide the river is about 40 yards wide at Axmouth, becoming very narrow at the mouth where the shifting shingle bank makes access difficult and often dangerous for fishing and other boats. The adjoining marshes are essential for maintaining the wader and waterbird population there at high-water, when the muddy shores are covered.

BIRDWATCHING BY TRAM

The Seaton Tramway which runs alongside the estuary of the Axe was built on an earlier floodbank constructed to reclaim marshland for grazing. Conservation and ornithological groups charter trams for birdwatching trips, particularly in winter, for the trams offer excellent views of the river and the surrounding marshes, meadowland and reedbeds, alive with many species of waders and wildfowl, which it would be impossible to observe in any other way.

OTHER OPPORTUNITIES FOR BIRDWATCHING

Birdwatching is indeed a major attraction, for the great advantage of the Axe estuary is the extreme ease with which the extensive views and teeming birdlife can be enjoyed. There is a footpath on the western boundary running up from the Harbour Road car park, and on the eastern side the Axmouth to Seaton road provides good views of the river, mudflats, the upper estuary and meadowland. Birds can be viewed from a parked roadside car, and near the Harbour Inn there is a viewing point, off the road with bench seats and an information board.

BIRDS TO LOOK FOR IN WINTER

A typical winter list might include SHELDUCK, WIGEON, TEAL, OYSTERCATCHER, LAPWING, DUNLIN, REDSHANK, CURLEW, HERON, RINGED PLOVER, LITTLE GREBE, CORMORANT, GREY PLOVER, SPOTTED REDSHANK, GREENSHANK, COMMON SANDPIPER, KINGFISHER and various types of GULL. Some of the rare birds seen in recent years include OSPREY, GREAT CRESTED GREBES, SMEWS, AVOCETS and LITTLE EGRETS. There are resident and wintering SWANS. BUZZARDS are often seen soaring overhead.

* * * * *

Mute Swans   *Curlew*

AXMOUTH

The clear waters of the gentle river Axe flow through the colourful, pastoral landscape of Dorset, Somerset and Devon to meet the sea at Axmouth, just east of the haven, and now slightly further upstream than Seaton. The quiet and pretty village which nestles beneath the ancient fortified Hawkesdown Hill, which was established as a settlement in Saxon times and bears signs of Roman activity, was once a busy port thronging with seafarers.

ITS EARLY HISTORY

Originally a property of the king since Anglo Saxon times, the Manor of Axmouth was given to Richard de Redvers after the Norman Conquest and was later made over to the Abbey of St Mary of Montebourg in Normandy and then transferred to an abbey in Isleworth, Middlesex. Records show that it was surrendered by the Abbess to King Henry VIII who left it to Queen Catherine for her lifetime and then to the boy King Edward VI. It was subsequently granted to Walter Earle who was 'one of the grooms of the privy chamber', in 1552. In the 17th century it passed on to Sir Walter Yonge, who sold it in 1691 to Richard Hallett of Lyme Regis, and it remained in the Hallett family until it passed to the Sanders Stephens family.

TRADERS AND SEAFARERS

A clear stream still ripples its charming way through the village alongside the road to join the main river at the once busy point known as Millmead. In former times part of the settlement was situated nearer the mouth of the river. When the port was at its height it was a very busy place, said to have as many as 14 inns, where many an old salt went to quench his thirst and spin a yarn or two with other seafarers. Today things are rather quieter down Axmouth way, and there are just two remaining inns, the Ship and the Harbour.

'AN OLDE AND BIGGE FISCHAR TOUNE'

In the 16th century the historian Leland wrote, 'I passed from Seton at ebbe over the salt marshes and the ryver Ax to Axmouth, an olde and bigge fischar toune on the est side of the Haven.'

CARGO CHARGES

The 1830 Act of George IV maintaining and governing the harbour had a comprehensive table of cargo charges ranging from 'Ale, Beer or Porter, per kilderkin' to 'Yarn of all sorts, per ton.' After the blocking of the harbour entrance there were repeated efforts to clear it and the port of Axmouth functioned on a restricted scale.

HAWKESDOWN HILL

The steeply rising Hawkesdown Hill, known variously as Hawkesdon, Hawksdown, 'Hockdown', 'Hocksdon', 'Hochsdun', probably stemming from the German 'hoch', meaning 'high' and 'dun' indicating a hill, is topped by an Ancient British hillfort built by the Durotriges in defence of rival tribes of the West Country. Local folk sometimes referred to it as 'Oxen 'ill'.

There are fine views from the top of Hawkesdown Hill and the other major forts of the Axe Valley can be seen from here. In olden times beacons were lit on hills such as this to warn of impending danger.

OLD NAMES

The port may have been known to the Romans by the name 'Uxelis', the name 'Alaenus' is thought to refer to the river Axe and 'Alaeni Ostia' would have been Axmouth.

ST. MICHAEL'S CHURCH

St. Michael's church with its square tower and quaint gargoyles, situated close to the corner of River Road is of Norman origin with some of the original work remaining, the north door and parts of the piers in the arcades being particularly good examples of those times. Around 1300 and 1500 there were considerable alterations when the arches on the south side of the nave were straightened, the east and north windows constructed and the tower rebuilt at the west end of the nave.

Inside the church are monuments to the Erle and Hallett families who were former lords of the manor.

Axmouth seen across the estuary

CANINE OR FELINE?

The story goes that the medieval effigy in the chancel, depicting a priest reclining with crossed hands, his head on a pillow and his feet resting on an animal — which could be a dog or a lion — results from a benefactor who performed good works on condition that his favourite pet dog was buried and immortalised with him, in death. This is linked to the legend of Dog Acre Orchard, which might well have originated as 'God Acre' Orchard. However, excavations revealed no trace of such a dog, and an alternative theory that the beast represents a lion and that it follows the theme of the 91st Psalm might be more likely: 'Thou shalt tread upon the lion and the adder, the young lion and dragon shalt thou trample under feet....' On the other hand some might look in vain for the adder and the dragon. After the Reformation there was a short lived fashion for incorporating family pets in this way with effigies.

THE CHURCHYARD

On the south side of the churchyard there is evidence of a mass burial, with a collection of bones too numerous to have been drawn from the immediate locality and it is considered likely to have been associated with those who fell in the fierce and bloody battle of Brunenburg between the invading Danes led by Anlaf and the Saxon King Athelstan.

THE OLD QUERN

An old quern, or handmill was taken from a farmhouse on Hawkesdown and mounted on the wall close to the gate of the church. It was a hollowed out stone with a spout on one side through which liquid might pass. As the spout was on one side only, it was thought that the stone might have served the dual purpose of cider press and corn crusher.

STEDCOMBE HOUSE

Ideally situated on the green and pastoral slopes on the eastern side of the Axe, the attractive and distinctive Stedcombe House, built in 1695, occupies the site of a former mansion which was burnt down during the Civil War. In 1644 it was garrisoned for Parliament by Sir Walter Erle and after an intense 3 hour assault on 22nd March of that year, it was taken over by a strong body of Royalist troops, who seized weapons and ammunition, then burnt the place down. The parish register contained entries pertaining to the burial of the casualties.

Back in the Middle Ages Stedcombe belonged to Gervais de Uffewill, then passed to the de Veres and the Courtenays, becoming a Crown property when that family got into difficulties. It was given to the Carews and passed to the Yonge family in 1551. It remained in that family for 140 years.

Having been rebuilt after the Civil War, around 1697 it was acquired by the Halletts of Lyme Regis who had made a fortune in the sugar and rum trade in the West Indies, thus earning a place amidst the County gentry. The interior was lavishly renovated in 1760 with much ornate wood carving and an elaborate rococo chimney piece was installed in the drawing room. From the outside it has a pleasing, equilateral appearance with its centrally placed chimney stack and neatly emphasised windows.

THE LOST COMMONLAND

The network of deep combes around the village which had traditionally been commonland were commandeered and fenced off by the Lord of Stedcombe Manor in 1905, arousing enormous resentment from the villagers.

IN FOR A PENNY

There were a number of estates around the area and the villagers would look on in awe as the gentry went about its affairs. When they arrived at the gates of the estate in their stylish, horse drawn carriages the local children would open the gates and rush to pick up the pennies which were thrown out for them.

STEPPES COTTAGES

The 15th century Steppes Cottages, now a Country Club was a mansion owned by the Mallock family until they moved to Rousdon in 1617. Later converted into 5 cottages for labourers, they re-assumed their former glory after being purchased by the Chappell family in 1932, with the original flagstones and fine oak beaming remaining intact.

COOMBE FARM

The ancient farmhouse, part of which was said to have been built by monks of Lodres Priory retains beautiful old panelling and fine oak beams, one of which was fashioned from the timbers of a wrecked ship. At the time of the unpopular 'window tax', four of the old windows were filled in.

SMUGGLING

The area around the landslip was ideal smuggling territory, well known to the notorious Jack Rattenbury. Signs would be left around the place, transmitting local 'intelligence' reports, and the expression 'the coast is clear' meant exactly what it said. Just such a secret communication system was housed in the wall of Coombe Farm, and contraband goods would be stored in cellars and hiding places around the area until it was safe to move it on.

Stedcombe House

21

COASTGUARDS

The presence of coastguards nearby did not seem to inhibit the illicit activity too much and very few smugglers were taken to task. When the coastguard station situated near Squire Lane and overlooking Axmouth Harbour was sold, the coastguards operated from the clifftop lookout above Beer.

CIDER MAKING

Axmouth was reputed to be the first place in Devonshire to make cider. Around 1286 it was said to be recognised as the staple drink for the farmworkers of the Manor.

Older village folk recall the childhood delights of scrumping in the orchards belonging to the farms, which made cider to be sold in flasks. These would be taken to the neighbouring inns to be poured straight from the flasks to the awaiting mugs.

FIRKINS AND DRINKING HORNS

Farm workers would take their firkins to the farmhouse to be filled up every morning before spending the day working in the fields. The village children who helped out on the land during the school holidays would be sent back to the farmhouse to refill the empty firkins. Farm labourers also used drinking horns which were easy to carry and easy to grip, and these were made from the hollowed out horns of cattle.

Grey Heron

FARMHOUSE CHEESES

Some of the farms in the Axe Valley would produce whole, round cheeses in various sizes which the menfolk would collect after the day's work and carry home in hessian sacks slung over their shoulders. A particular favourite was a white cheese which later went blue, which was produced on a farm over at Colyton.

DUCKS' DELIGHT

In 1875 the village was idyllically described as being situated in the midst of orchards, fields, hedges and trees. It was said to consist of, 'two very pleasant streets, through which flows a beautiful little stream, in all its freshness from the fountains of the hills, and never failing as the habitat of endless ducks.' Francis Bickley wrote in 1911: 'Down one long street of cottages wanders a brooklet of crystal clear water, the playground of the cleanest ducks in the world.' Sadly, the motor cars which speed through the village these days leave no scope for ducks.

Axmouth Village

23

EFFERVESCENT WATER

There are a number of springs around the area, and Axmouth is to be envied for the pure qualities of its effervescent water. Springhead water issues from the floor of the steep-sided valley, a short way up from the east of the village. Coming from chalk, it has a high calcium content.

MODERN ROADS

Around the beginning of this century the uneven, muddy and rutted cart tracks gave way to well surfaced, well drained roads constructed of carefully graded stones, which were broken up to the correct size.

RIVER ROAD

Before the New Road was built alongside the estuary of the Axe, there was a rough road which regularly flooded and at extra high tide was impassable. Horse drawn carts were taken through the water at high tide while cyclists took the adjoining footpath through the fields, lifting their cycles over the stiles and 'kissing gates' along the way. River Road, built in 1928 is still referred to as 'New' Road, by the local people, and it has been of great value to local folk and visitors who possibly take it for granted these days. A guidebook written in 1912 states: 'For some time the authorities have had under consideration the question of raising the road, and in some way remedying the present state of affairs, but the expense will be very great and the matter is still in abeyance. When the work is carried out it will doubtless be a great boon to people of Axmouth as well as to those whose business or pleasure take them in that direction.'

CLIFFSLIDE

Local folk recall a huge cliff fall at Haven Cliff about 60 years ago when the cliff subsided and gouged the undercliff into the sea, causing the clifftop coastguard hut to topple onto the beach. It took a couple of winters for the fallen rocks to be washed away by wave action.

AXMOUTH'S INNS

Old records claim that Axmouth, anciently a place of great importance, being part of the Anglo Saxon royal demesne could boast of 14 hotels. Francis Bickley who wrote the entertaining and readable book WHERE DORSET MEETS DEVON, published in 1911 made the comment, 'Anglo Saxon *hotels* tickles the fancy.'

Today Axmouth has just two inns, recalling its seafaring associations in their names, the Ship and the Harbour Inns. The previous Ship Inn burnt down on Christmas Day in 1875.

BURNING THE ASHEN FAGGOT

The Harbour Inn still follows the old custom of Burning the Ashen Faggot on Christmas Eve, whereby the bundle of ashwood secured with binds and known as the 'faggot' is put on the open fire. Every time the bind cracks it is time to buy another drink.

THREE TRUSTS

Today three village 'Trusts' survive. There is the Davis Trust, the Searles Charity given from Dowlands and now administered by the Parish Council for educational purposes and the Dares Charity for widows and widowers.

AXMOUTH TODAY

Today the village is a mixture of carefully restored old cottages and more recent development with two inns, a church, a disused school which now functions as the village hall and the friendly Post Office/General Stores, run variously by the Reals, the Spillers and the Baters. The village has certainly seen some changes since Saxon times. Modern day Axmouth is a place where locals and newcomers with a variety of backgrounds blend in well together, united in their pride and interest in their historic and beautiful environment.

A clear stream still ripples its charming way along the sides of the roads to join the main river at Millmead. The seafarers have long departed and the ducks have gone. The estuary has become a valued haven for the wildlife now, thus fulfilling a modern need, undreamed of when the world was younger.

* * * * *

BINDON HOUSE

About half a mile east of the village is the beautifully situated, picturesque 15th century Bindon Manor House which incorporates a chapel of an earlier date and probably occupies the site of an older building. Once owned by Nicholas Bach, it was sold in the reign of Henry IV to Roger Wyke who had the chapel licensed by Bishop Lacy on 16th July 1425. Through heiresses it came into the part ownership of the Gifford, Barry and Erle families, and the Erle family, originally from Somerset made Bindon their home. A descendant, Sir Walter Erle was knighted in 1616, became member of Parliament for Lyme Regis in 1625 and was an active Parliamentarian during the Civil War. He also made efforts to repair the haven, but the project was abandoned after his death. The house was also in the ownership of the Rowe, Southcott, Hallett and Chappell families, and in 1890 the Chappells sold Bindon to the Smedmore Estate, and it was later sold again.

THE BARN AND THE WELL

In the courtyard is the fine, old manorial barn with crenellated openings, and a deep, very old well from which water used to be drawn with the assistance of a wheel.

THE 'CLINK' LINK

Old records indicate that the building at one time was generally known as 'Jail Court' and further mention of chains fastened to the walls and floors adds to the likelihood of the place having been used to house prisoners.

THE OLD SHEEP WASH

The old sheep wash, situated near the entrance to the estate was itself washed away in the floods of 1960.

THE OLD WATER SUPPLY

In olden times local villagers used to fetch and carry their water each day from the Bindon springs on the estate. Cattle were also driven there daily to be watered. The water, which is reputed to have therapeutic properties was said to be particularly beneficial for sore eyes.

THE WITHY BEDS AND WATERCRESS BEDS

The young wood from the withy beds at Bindon was used for making hurdles for penning sheep, and watercress was also grown in the wet areas nearby.

* * * * *

ROUSDON

A mile or so to the east, and just inland of the landslip is the little village of Rousdon, described by the early historian Risdon as 'lying open to the sea.' Although there was so much water nearby and in the rocks beneath it, there had been some difficulty in the area of actually harnessing this vast supply and very deep wells had to be constructed.

THE NAME

The name probably stemmed from the former landowning family of Down or Donne, who favoured the tradition of handing down the name 'Ralph' to their sons. Hence the name 'Ralph' Down became corrupted to Rous Down and Rousdon. The Mallock family moved from Steppes House, Axmouth to Rousdon in 1617.

The original little old chapel at Rousdon had been quadrangular and thatched, but when Sir Henry William Peek, of 'biscuit' fame moved there he made sweeping changes and virtually had the village rebuilt. The church was replaced by another in 1871. The fine mansion incorporated Silician marble from a ship which was wrecked on rocks at the foot of the Landslip.

The lovely mansion now houses Allhallows School.

* * * * *

THE LANDSLIP

The famous Landslip which extends from Seaton to Lyme Regis is a unique area particularly interesting to geologists and naturalists, and it has been a National Nature Reserve since 1955. There is a footpath through the reserve which can be joined just east of the bridge at Axmouth, leading the seven miles or so to Lyme Regis.

THE GEOLOGY AND LANDSLIDES

The rock formations exposed in the cliffs in the area of the Landslip, east of Seaton include the Blue Lias, consisting of many alternating layers of Limestone and Shale and capped by thick Marls. The rock formations dip seawards and each ledge corresponds with a layer of Limestone. Water seeping through the intervening clays emerges as springs, which lubricate the rocks and wash out the sediment thus weakening the upper cliff and causing subsidence. The thick Marls and Clays which expand and contract with varying weather conditions, are also weakened and eventually collapse.

PINHAY BAY

There is a fault at Pinhay Bay, marked by a gully cut out by a stream which trickles down the steep slope, and buries itself in the rock debris. West of the fault the high cliffs have a capping of Chalk and Upper Greensand, seen in the breakaway at the edge of the plateau between Ware and Axmouth, and beneath this breakaway is a tract of tumbled and broken rock pinnacles and blocks of subsided Chalk with rifts and chasms.

LANDSLIDES AT DOWLANDS AND BINDON

There has been intermittent landsliding here for many centuries, with a big fall at Whitlands following a very wet year. However, the most dramatic landslide occurred at Dowlands on Christmas Eve 1839 when about 20 acres of land subsided carrying with it cottages, fields and hedgerows leaving a ravine 150 feet deep and 300 feet wide, and forcing land ahead of it into the sea. Offshore a mile long reef was forced up about 40 feet high, but it subsided shortly afterwards. Astonishingly, one cottage was borne along with events to arrive near the shore more or less intact, and the crops in the transported fields were harvested the following year when there were great celebrations and people came from far and wide to look and wonder.

The Landslip of 1839

27

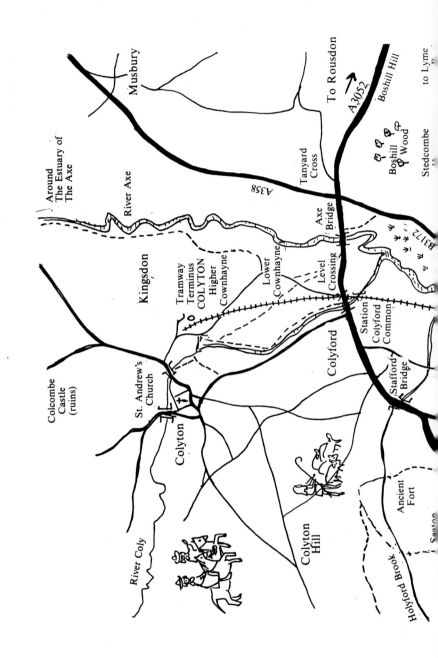

Around
The Estuary of
The Axe

Musbury

River Axe

A358

Tanyard Cross

To Rousdon

A3052

Boshill Hill

to Lyme

Boshill Wood

Stedcombe

Axe Bridge

B3172

Kingsdon

Tramway Terminus
COLYTON

Higher Cownhayne

Lower Cownhayne

Level Crossing

Station

Colyford Common

Colyford

Stafford Bridge

Colcombe Castle (ruins)

St. Andrew's Church

Colyton

River Coly

Colyton Hill

Ancient Fort

Holyford Brook

Seaton

28

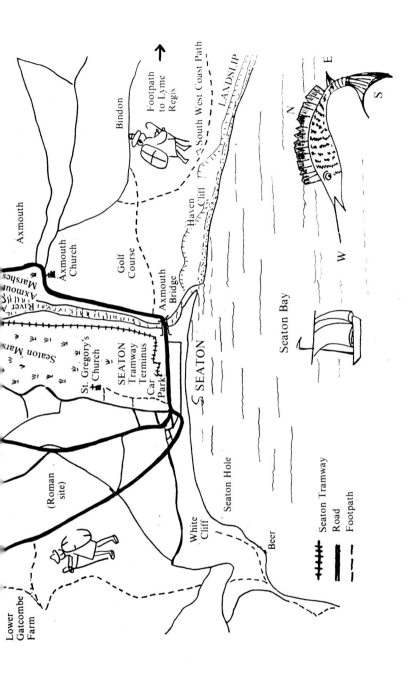

Axmouth

Bindon

Footpath
to Lyme
Regis

South West Coast Path

LANDSLIP

Axmouth
Church

Golf
Course

Haven
Cliff

Axmouth
Bridge

River Axe

Axmouth
Marshes

Seaton Marshes

St. Gregory's
Church

SEATON
Tramway
Terminus

Car
Park

SEATON

Seaton Bay

(Roman
site)

White
Cliff

Seaton Hole

Beer

Lower
Gatcombe
Farm

Seaton Tramway

Road

Footpath

N

E

S

W

THE NATIONAL NATURE RESERVE

A combination of sunny, southerly aspect, an abundant seepage of water on the tumbled mass of Chalk, Sandstones and Clays, with instability and inaccessibility has created a unique and very valuable ecological environment of great scientific interest. In these humid conditions, native plants flourish and grow to a great size, creating a dense, jungle-like pattern of vegetation.

THE NATURE CONSERVANCY COUNCIL

The Nature Conservancy Council is anxious to seek the public's co-operation in safeguarding the reserve from fires, litter and the removal of specimens. Information pamphlets can be obtained from the Tourist Information Centre on the front at Seaton.

HEIGHT OF THE SEASON BUS SERVICE FOR WALKERS

During the height of the summer holiday season, special buses operate between Seaton and Lyme Regis which are particularly convenient for those wishing to enjoy the Landslip walk.

* * * * *

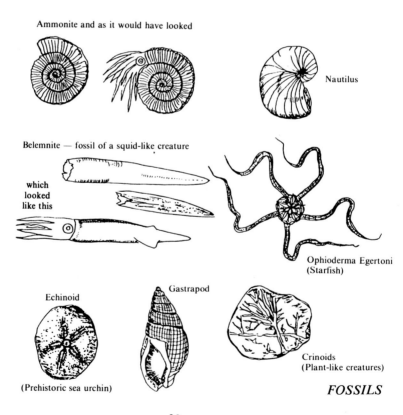

Ammonite and as it would have looked

Nautilus

Belemnite — fossil of a squid-like creature

which looked like this

Ophioderma Egertoni
(Starfish)

Echinoid

Gastrapod

Crinoids
(Plant-like creatures)

(Prehistoric sea urchin)

FOSSILS

COLYFORD AND COLYTON

About two miles to the north of Seaton the River Axe is joined by the River Coly, and the village of Colyford is situated where the old Dorchester to Exeter road forded the River Coly. Situated on the main Roman thoroughfare, it was once a place of importance and much bigger; or as an early historian wrote in 1724, 'here have been many inns and a considerable town.' Colyford was a borough town, having been constituted by a Royal Charter obtained by a member of the Bassett family, a former Lord of Colyton. Now a village and a borough in name only, it still elects a Mayor, Clerk, Mace Bearer and Constable.

THE SHAKESPEARE CONNECTION

Colyford was the birthplace of Sir Thomas Gates, who became Governor of Virginia in 1609, and who was shipwrecked with Sir George Somers, discovering the Bermudas by being washed up on those shores. Sir George Somers took possession of the Islands in the name of the King, thereby introducing the name 'Somer's Islands'. This rather unlikely and colourful incident is said to have inspired Shakespeare's play *The Tempest*.

COLYTON

The handsome town of Colyton, dating from early Saxon times enjoys a splendid situation on the green and pleasant banks of the gentle River Coly, set amidst the watermeadows and sheltered by dark green, rolling hills. The old, stylish and well cared for buildings, now in a conservation area, line the compact streets of seemingly haphazard, but interesting lay-out. This tight design was functional in that the town could be readily closed off for defensive purposes.

With a population of around 2,000, Colyton is the smallest town in Devon. There is a strong community spirit and the townsfolk are justifiably proud of the town's widespread reputation of it being a very friendly place.

EARLY HISTORY

Dating back to Saxon times and possibly even earlier, Colyton was part of the West Saxon Royal demesne given by William the Conqueror to Robert de Mount Chardon at the time of the Conquest. During the reign of Richard I it came into the possession of the Bassett family, passing to the Earls of Devon before being confiscated by the Crown in 1538, when Henry Courtenay who had fallen out of Royal favour was executed. It was later restored to that family by Queen Mary and it was subsequently sold to William Pole.

YEARLY FAIR

In 1208 King John granted to Thomas Bassett a Seven Day Fair to be held at the Feast of St. Michael. By 1838 there were three weekly markets and two yearly fairs.

Today the well supported Colyton Carnival is recognised as one of the best events of its type throughout the area.

'THE CHAUNTRYE CALLED THE COLYFORD CHAUNTRYE...'

There was formerly a chantry chapel near Colyford Bridge, mentioned in the Chantry Roll of 1547 but no trace of the building remains. It was stated that 'The Chauntrye called Colyford Chauntrye, founded by the Erle of Devon for the perpetuall fynding of a pryste to mynystre dyvyne servyce in a chapple of Saynt Edmunde, founded in the borough of Colyforde within the parysshe of Colyton, being distant from the parysshe church....'

The Church of St Michael was built as a Chapel-of-ease to the Mother Church at Colyton.

COLYFORD BRIDGE AND THE FOOTPATH ACROSS THE FIELDS

Colyford Bridge built in the middle of the 19th century replaced an older bridge dated 1681. There is a delightful walk through the watermeadows to Kingsdon and Colyton which starts almost opposite the White Hart Inn.

ST. ANDREW'S CHURCH

St. Andrew's Church with its square tower and its handsome and distinctive octagonal lantern is a pleasing landmark from miles around. Lower parts of the tower and the east end of the chancel are the oldest parts of the church, but it dates mostly from the 15th and 16th centuries. The tower, with its lantern has caused problems at various times in that the weight of it affected the foundations. At the end of the 18th century the tower was underpinned and the foundations rebuilt. The great perpendicular west window was rebuilt in 1902, unveiled two years later and completed in 1911. Appropriately, it depicted scenes from the life of St. Andrew.

Chantry Bridge over the Coly, Colyton

"LITTLE CHOKE-A-BONE'

The Courtenay monument which was removed from the north transept to the chancel in 1818 and popularly known as 'Little Choke-A-Bone' particularly stirred the romantic imagination of the Victorians. Depicting a recumbant figure of a girl wearing a coronet resting her head on an angel and her feet on a dog, it was reputed to have been Margaret, daughter of William Courtenay, who 'died at Colcombe, choked by a fish bone.' Historians differ as to the accuracy of this inscription, some saying that if that young lady ever had a problem with a fishbone that she must have overcome it enough to grow up and marry Lord Henry Herbert, or that the coat of arms is of a married woman, Margaret, daughter of John Beaufort, Earl of Somerset and wife of Thomas, 5th Earl of Devon, whom she married in 1431. The wrong inscription may have come about as a result of moving the monument. On the other hand, George P. R. Pulman, who wrote the prestigious Book of the Axe maintains that the tale of Little Choke-a-Bone is true.

OTHER MONUMENTS

This most attractive and interesting church bears witness to the powerful, landowning families including the Poles, Yonges, Courtenays and Erles, who not only influenced life around these parts, but helped to shape our country's history.

Colyton Church

33

THE SAXON CROSS

The well preserved Saxon Cross dating from about A.D. 900 which stands in the south transept bears exquisite carving and has a strange history. During restoration work which followed the disastrous fire of 1933 it was noticed that some peculiarly shaped stones were embedded in the fabric of the tower. Further investigations revealed them to be sections of a Saxon Cross. Having been extricated and fitted together it is recognised as one of the best preserved examples in the country. Part of the original crosspiece remains missing, so it seems that the old tower has yet to reveal all its secrets.

THE BELLS OF COLYTON TOWN

In the tower were six bells which formed one of the heaviest peals of six in the county. One of the bells is inscribed:
>'When I call,
>Follow me all!'

THE FEOFFEES

The ancient word 'feoffees' denotes persons who are trustees of investments related to lands or estates. The Colyton Chamber of Feoffees originated in the reign of Henry VIII, after Henry Courtenay's execution when the Estate was seized by the Crown. Well-to-do citizens of the town, mostly merchants and yeomen raised 1,000 marks to purchase back part of the confiscated Manor of Colyton, the residue of the money being put in trust in order that it be used for good and commendable purposes. The ancient charter testifying to the original transaction, dated January 6th, 1546 is still in the town's possession, and the good work of the Feoffees continues to this day. Feoffees founded Colyton Grammar School now occupying a site at nearby Colyford, and still proudly carrying on its fine traditions.

The Chamber of Feoffees built the Feoffees Town Hall in 1927 on the site of the old market. Built in the Tudor style of red brick and Beer stone, it is a much appreciated asset to the town where dancing, concerts and a variety of local events are held. Earlier projects included provision for a water supply, street lighting, forming a fire brigade, renovation work, helping the needy and other deserving causes.

INTERESTING BUILDINGS

THE GERRARD ARMS, originally built of flint and cob but later renovated with a red brick facing was a former coaching inn. The stylish COLYTON HOUSE, built in the early 17th century, constructed of brick, stone and slate was reputed to have had a high wall built to protect a former mistress of the house from admiring male gazes. THE VICARAGE, built in 1529 by Dr Brerwode was described by Leland, the early historian as 'a fair house'. It has a Tudor front, Tudor panelling inside and an Elizabethan entrance hall, THE OLD SUNDAY SCHOOL, a two storey flintstone building was erected in the late 1830s from funds made available by the National Society for Promoting the Education of the Poor, and was administered by six trustees. The original Trust Deed is still held in the church. Although the church and the town used the building from time to time, it came into the possession of the Parochial Church Council in 1978. Having been used as a Sunday School and a school, it housed Colyton Grammar School until it moved to its new site at Colyford in 1928. Restored in recent years it is used again as a Sunday School and by various church groups. THE GREAT HOUSE, built by the Yonge family in the reign of James I was where the Duke of Monmouth was entertained on his journey westwards in 1680. He may well have set the style for other important people to come and settle in the town, but this association with the Duke of Monmouth was to have far reaching effects on the citizens at a later date. OROOLONG HOUSE, owned in the 18th century by Captain Henry Wilson was named after the island in which he was shipwrecked. COOMBE HOUSE, KINGDON COTTAGE, CHURCH HOUSE, THE OLD BAKEHOUSE and THE FORGE are amongst the many other buildings of interest and beauty to be seen around the town. The interesting historical features discovered in the premises of Bevis & Beckingsale may be viewed by appointment in office hours.

INNS

In common with a number of other places in the neighbourhood Colyton and Colyford had many inns at one time which included THE WHITE HART, THE DOLPHIN, SEVEN STARS, GERRARD'S ARMS, THE BEAR, THE GEORGE, THE COMPASSES, THE RED LION and the GLOBE (now the KINGFISHER).

STREET NAMES

Tradition is very much to the fore in the street names which included North, South, East and West as well as Fore and Church. King Street and Queen Street offer that extra touch of class, while Cuckoo Street, and Rosemary Lane have a poetic ring about them. The Butts were earth embankments, usually situated just outside a town for practising archery. Colyton men were also famous for their wrestling prowess.

COLCOMBE CASTLE

The remains of Colcombe Castle are situated some way out of the town, over Umborne Bridge beyond Colyton Station and the section of dismantled railway. Approached through a gateway with an attendant gatehouse, a later house, now a farmhouse was built on the site of the castle, incorporating parts of the older structure. The first building was erected by Hugh, Lord Courtenay, an early member of that ancient and influential family who was Baron of Okehampton in 1280. The property remained in that family until 1538 when it was seized by the Crown and then it passed successively to the Erles, the Drakes and the Poles, who restored it but then discarded the place in preference to nearby Shute House, now in the care of the National Trust. The Pole family, now residing in Cornwall are still Lords of the Manor of Colyton.

THE CIVIL WAR AND STRIFE

Colyton was quite a battleground during the Civil War, situated as it was between the territories of the Royalist Axminster and the Parliamentary garrison of Lyme. In 1644 there were many skirmishes through these narrow streets, 'the enemy was chased through Colliton Towne' and Colyton Bridge was captured and recaptured several times. The Parish Register contains references to the burial of those killed. Of the leading families the Poles were Royalists and the Erles were Parliamentarians. The townsfolk tended to favour the Parliamentarian cause and dragoons were stationed there in 1685, probably as a result of the town's earlier associations with the Duke of Monmouth. Followers from Colyton rushed to join Monmouth's rebel band when they heard of his landing at Lyme.

RETRIBUTION AND THE PLAGUE

After the uprisings the hunt was on for supporters of the cause and suspects. A man named Clapp who lived at a house known as The Bird Cage, long since burnt down was in bed when he heard the approach of the King's men and with great presence of mind hopped nimbly up through the trapdoor in the ceiling and hid in the roof. A warm bed provided proof of his recent departure, but failing to track him down they continued on their way to root out easier prey. Another fugitive living at Bull's Court was with his family as soldiers approached. Diving in amongst the cabbages growing in the garden, he might well have escaped their attentions, had not one of his young children innocently betrayed him. The story goes that he was seized and executed on the spot. After the notorious Bloody Assizes those found guilty by Judge Jeffreys were subjected to harsh brutality and even those executed were subjected to further humiliation in death by being decapitated and quartered, with sections of their bodies being strewn around all over the place. Colyton folk were numbered among those so treated.

A number of townsfolk had also suffered from looting and rough treatment at the hands of the dragoons who were stationed there in 1685; William Bird, a silk mercer and John Hewes, being two victims who were later recompensed.

The plague had hit the town at various times, the worst outbreak being in 1645/6.

ANCIENT TRACKWAYS AND FARMSTEADS

Cargoes of salt drawn by packhorses made their way to inland centres through narrow lanes which came to be known as 'saltways'. 'Whit' indicates a connection with the salt trade, hence Whitwell and Whitford. Salters Lane, at the back of Colyford is likely to have been on one of these routes. Narrow Devonshire lanes which are such a delight today, with their high hedges and profusion of wild flowers originally linked the ancient farm enclosures.

The word 'Barton' indicates a farmyard in the case of a farm not being let with the rest of the manor. Many farmsteads around this immediate locality incorporate the word 'hayes' or 'hayne' in their names, prefixed by a personal name. 'Hayes' or 'hayne' were Medieval English words for hay.

TRADITIONAL INDUSTRIES AND CRAFTS

Colyton was formerly an important centre for the West of England cloth trade which suffered a decline when the industrial north cornered the market. There were paper mills, saw mills, corn mills and a small iron foundry. The town produced fine pillow lace and local farms were noted for their cheese and cider making. Today the tannery still uses the traditional oak bark method of tanning hides for leather to be used for specialist medical purposes, and there is a technical components factory in the town. Aware of the traditions, craftsmen have been attracted to the area. Thus woodcrafts, saddlery and leather crafts, wrought iron work, brasswork and other specialised crafts are flourishing.

SEATON TRAMWAY

At one time Colyton and Colyford enjoyed the advantages of being linked to the main London to Exeter railway line and down the branch line to Seaton, but the line was an early casualty of the Beeching pruning. However, in the spring of 1980 the Seaton Tramway extended their route over the level crossing at Colyford to terminate at Colyton. The trams are a valued amenity for local people who can use them all the year round to travel down to Seaton. All-weather trams are in use on the line.

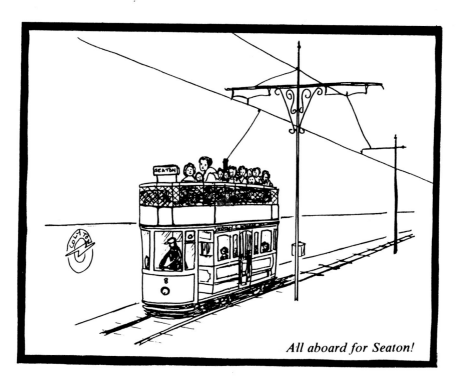

All aboard for Seaton!

37

Pillow lace making was a cottage industry in local villages.

AXE BRIDGE

The modern Axe Bridge which carries the A3052 over that river replaced the bridge built for wheeled carriages in 1837, which in its turn replaced a much loved, picturesque stone bridge of which it was written:

'An auntient bridge of stone
A goodly work when first it was reared.'

The jutting masonry, designed to alleviate flooding helped to create a type of weir which trapped fish and prevented the salmon from getting any further upstream.

MUSBURY AND THE CHURCH

The nearby village of Musbury, anciently known as Muchbury, was a Courtenay property before the Reformation and owned by the Drake family afterwards. Inside the interesting and attractive old church with its low, massive tower is a very unusual triple monument erected to the Drake family in 1611, consisting of effigies of three armoured knights of that family, kneeling beside their wives in prayer.

BEER

The ancient and charming fishing village of Beer, situated about a mile to the west of Seaton lies in a sheltered little bay, in a deep combe, dominated by the colourful towering cliffs. An old guidebook published in 1865 stated enthusiastically that 'the traveller will be charmed by this romantic village on his descent from the cliffs. It is situated in a little glen, and a stream runs merrily through it, leaping to the sea in a cascade.'

'AN HAMLET OF FISCHARMEN'

Back in the Middle Ages it had been described as 'an hamlet of fischarmen', when there had been attempts to build a pier. Unfortunately 'there came such a tempest as never in mind of man had before been seen in that shore, and tore the pier to pieces.'

'TWO OR THREE FAIR INNS'

At the end of the 19th century it was recorded that 'Beer consists mainly of a long, straggling street threading a narrow valley upwards from the sea, and containing two or three fair inns.'

THE WAYSIDE STREAM

The clear, sparkling water which ripples alongside the road, eager to find the sea, and which formerly cascaded over the rocks, was harnessed to work a mill at one time.

THE VILLAGE TODAY

Some of the picturesque, thatched cottages were replaced by villas when the Rolle family set about upgrading standards in the village, and modern buildings and new housing development has crept up the sides of the combes. But Beer has retained much of its earlier character and charm and the local fishermen from well established seafaring families go about their traditional way of life much as they have always done.

HOW DID IT GET ITS NAME?

The unusual name of 'Beer' arouses curiosity and there are a number of theories as to how the village came by it. Ancient records mention Berham or Bereham, which would indicate a hamlet of barley ricks. By the time of the Middle Ages it was known as Brerword. Alternatively the name Beer may stem from the Norse word 'byr' meaning a farmstead, and nearby places west of the Axe incorporate the word 'bere' or 'beer' in their names. Or it may be from the Anglo-Saxon 'bearo', meaning scrub woodland of the fruit bearing kind. Yet another theory is that 'B' was prefixed to earr, ear, or, and ur, which anciently described coastal characteristics.

EARLY HISTORY

In 1005 Beer was incorporated in the land given by King Aethelred to Eadsig, the haven of Beer then being known by the name Shipcombe. On the death of Eadsig it passed to the Priory of Horton in East Dorset and on to Sherborne Abbey in 1122. At that time the south facing slopes were used for vineyards, the wine being used for hospitality as well as sacramental purposes. The village also produced fodder, fish and salt, and at the time of Domesday there were four salt works.

Together with Seaton it passed after the Dissolution to Catherine Parr, and was sold to the Hassard family of Lyme and then to John Starre, whose house was at the top of the village and who was buried in the churchyard at Seaton. In 1630 it was in the possession of the Walronds of Bovey and through marriage it passed to Lord Rolle. The manor was later held by Lord Clinton.

THE PLAGUE

When the dreaded plague hit the village it wiped out about three quarters of the population; the graveyard of the old chapel was filled and has never been opened since. The chapel was later pulled down.

THE SPANISH CONNECTION

Shortly afterwards it is said that a Spanish vessel was wrecked on rocks in Beer Cove and that the Spanish sailors found a welcome in the depopulated village. They set about repopulating the village with great enthusiasm, and the more discerning observer might detect Andalusian features in the locality today.

LACE MAKING

Following a 16th century massacre in the Netherlands refugee families who came to settle on the South Devon coast brought with them their tradition of Flemish handicrafts, particularly lace making, which flourished around Honiton, Beer and the little villages round and about. Reputed for its fine workmanship and high quality it was finished over hard, hay stuffed pillows with the pattern pricked out by pins on pieces of waxed paper. The extremely fine cotton thread of 140 or 160 gauge was worked with wooden bobbins, and women toiled away in their cottage doorways, nimble fingers flying with great dexterity. There were exquisite displays of lacework in Beer shop windows.

BY ROYAL APPOINTMENT

Queen Victoria's wedding dress, 'beautiful beyond description' was made from Beer lace and cost £1,000. There has been subsequent royal patronage.

GUNFLINTS

A rather less dainty product, but requiring nimble fingers and a deft hand nevertheless were gunflints, manufactured from the material found in the chalk cliffs. There was a knack to fashioning a perfectly shaped flint. Gunflints were produced on contract to the Army and the Navy as well as being sold to private individuals.

BOVEY HOUSE

Bovey House, now in use as a hotel is situated about a mile to the north west of Beer. Built in the Elizabethan style it was approached through a long avenue of lime trees. Belonging to the Walrond family since the reign of Henry III it was described in 1790 as having 'something unusually striking in the antique mansion, the old rookery behind it, the mossy pavement of the court, the raven in the porch, grey with years, and even the domestics hoary in service. They were all grown old together, and this co-incidence was peculiarly interesting.' A perceptive description, giving insight into the characters, their way of life and the writer, and proving that human nature does not change all that much despite social changes.

The well, 180 feet deep was once used as a hiding place, for there was a 10 foot square chamber about 30 feet down, probably for the safety of the person cleaning out the well. A secret hiding place was discovered in one of the chimneys.

Bovey House and the lane leading to it were said to have been haunted. This may have been a useful ploy to discourage people from the vicinity, thus leaving greater scope for the smugglers' activities.

42

THE ROLLE FAMILY

The Rolle family moved into Devonshire and purchased considerable lands of the dismantled abbeys. The family performed good works around the village, and Lady Judith Maria Rolle was particularly remembered for her charitable acts, including the founding of almshouses and schools. The almshouses were 'for the use of twenty eight poor and infirm fishermen above fifty five years and twenty poor women of the same age, each of whom receives a shilling a week for life, with other benefits.'

OTHER CHARITIES

In 1801, Mr. Edward Good of Beer and the Rev. Robert Cutcliffe gave £20, with which the interest would provide money for the poor of Seaton and Beer of which a third went to Seaton folk and two thirds to the folk of Beer. In 1733 Robert Marwood Esq. left twenty shillings a year to the poor of Beer.

ARTISTS

Not surprisingly, the charm of the village, the attraction of the shore, the quality of the light and the diversity of the colours has long attracted artists to the area. In a green enclosure above the beach is a memorial to the artist Hamilton Macallum, who lived in Beer for many years and died in 1896.

THE PROPOSED CANAL

The proposed construction of a ship canal from Beer to Stolford, linking the English Channel to the Bristol Channel, was approved by Act of Parliament and Telford was appointed as engineer. The tremendous enthusiasm for the project rapidly evaporated at the prospect of trying to raise the one and three quarter million pounds that was needed to finance it.

JACK RATTENBURY

Rather strangely, perhaps, the notorious smuggler Jack Rattenbury was called to London to advise on the prospect of creating the new canal. Obviously delighted at the idea of extending his professional activities to the north Somerset shores in this way 'he returned home with blue ribbons in his hat and a merry heart, from the expectation of deriving great advantages from the passing of the act....' It must have wiped the smile from his face when he learnt that the project was being abandoned.

Jack Rattenbury had to withdraw from his smuggling career — as a result of gout! He ended his days respectably, doing contract work for Blue Lias Lime at Sidmouth Harbour. His subsequent pension of a shilling a week, courtesy of Lord Rolle must have come in handy.

SMUGGLING

The indented coastline around Beer was ideal for smuggling activity which thrived in these parts. Very few smugglers were caught or punished, mainly due to the ineffectual and lax coastguards and excisemen, who often had a 'finger in the pie' themselves. At one time it was said that all the Beer trawlers were involved with contraband goods.

Fishing boats at Beer

There were many swashbuckling and adventurous stories concerning the exploits of the smugglers, which were romantic and stirred the imagination. Jack Rattenbury, never slow to spot an opportunity cashed in on the situation and had the audacity to print a book in Sidmouth in 1837 entitled: 'Memoirs of a Smuggler, compiled from his Diary and Journal: containing the Principal Events in the life of John Rattenbury, of Beer, Devonshire; commonly called 'the Rob Roy of the West.' In the book he tells us of experiencing 'the greatest vicissitudes, my spirits having been alternately elated by success, or depressed by misfortune, but in the midst of the whole I never yielded to despair, for hope was the pole star which shed its cheering rays, and illuminated my path in the darkest storm of adversity.' Some historians question whether a smuggler and rogue could possibly have such a command of language, and who might have been behind the writing of such a book.

Smugglers are always related to times gone by. A guidebook of 1865 stated that the area was 'in times past a nest of the most incorrigible smugglers.' At the time that was written the local smugglers were having a field day.

POINTS OF PARTICULAR INTEREST

The nave, transepts and porch are of 13th century origin. There is Saxon herringbone chiselling in the base of the tower which has a graceful, rounded Norman turret. The central chamber of the tower was a priests' room. Also of particular interest is the fine Elizabethan oak gallery and the rare three decker pulpit. The lowest level was where the Lesson was read, the middle was for saying the prayers and the most elevated position was where the sermons were preached; all of which must have been good for the morale of the preacher looking down, with some advantage over his flock.

In 'Branscombe Revisited' Eden Phillpotts wrote:
'On her green nest your Mother Church
Still spreads grey wings above her graves.'

THE CHURCHYARD

The captain and crewmen of the Danish frigate Ornen, wrecked off the coast on December 3rd 1802 are buried in the churchyard. In that incident 10 men and a boy were rescued.

Branscombe Church

FROM HERE TO ETERNITY ....

The records tell of Thomas Gilbart Smith MD, FRCP, who, 'after watching the glorious sunset of August 3rd 1902, fell dead from his bicycle,' and of the exciseman who fell from the cliffs whilst trying to extinguish a clifftop fire which had been lit as a signal for smugglers offshore.

CHURCH LIVING

Church Living, almost opposite the church is said to be one of the earliest inhabited medieval houses in the country. It was built by Bishop Bronescombe, who built part of Exeter Cathedral.

SOME ANCIENT HOUSES AND IMPORTANT FAMILIES

EDGE BARTON, formerly Egge and sometimes referred to as Edge was a property held by the Bronescombes or De Branscombe family from the time of the Norman Conquest until the time of Edward III, when it passed to the Wadham family. It was the birthplace of Walter Branscombe, a 13th century Bishop of Exeter who was remembered as a great builder, having built the Lady Chapel of Exeter Cathedral and adjoining chapels and played an inspirational part in other buildings, including the fine church at Ottery St. Mary. Three of that family became Sheriffs to the County of Devon. The Wadhams, Wyndhams and Strangways families later resided there. Joan Wadham, twice married, bore 20 children including Nicholas Wadham, who with his wife founded Wadham College, Oxford.

Branscombe

50

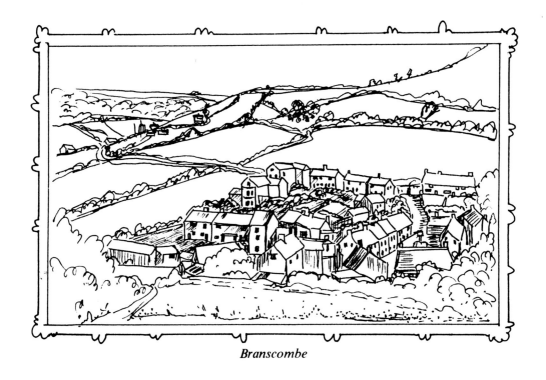

Branscombe

HOLE, a late 16th century house was originally the seat of the Holcombes, passing in the 17th century to the Bartletts and then the Stuckeys. Justice Stuckey had the rare distinction of being able to strike terror into the hearts of the local smuggling fraternity. The house has a fine Elizabethan fireplace still bearing the carved signatures of three members of the Holcombe family.

LOWER HOUSE, in the possession of the Ford family since the 16th century was visited by the Grand Duchess Helene of Russia in 1831 when she stayed in Sidmouth for some months.

BERRY BARTON, also known as Bury Barton and mentioned in 1307 as 'La Biry', situated near ancient earthworks was rebuilt in 1887 after a fire. It was said to be haunted by a little old woman who was murdered there and there is also a strange tale about a ghostly lady in red with a tall hat and buckled shoes who searched for a hidden hoard, obviously hoping to belie the popularly held view that you can't take it with you!

BARNELLS, formerly named Trafalgar House, having been built by Captain Yule, who served aboard the Victory at Trafalgar enjoys a particularly enviable situation. MARGEL'S COTTAGE, THE OLD FORGE, THE MASONS ARMS and THE THREE HORSESHOES are among other interesting old buildings to be savoured.

LEGENDS

THE LEGEND OF ST. WINIFRED

According to the ancient legend St. Winifred was loved by Prince Cradocus, who felt slighted as she did not encourage his attentions. In a fit of pique he cut off her head which rolled away down the hillside, whereupon swift heavenly retribution caused him to drop down dead and be swallowed up by the earth. Meanwhile St. Bueno, who happened to be out for a stroll at the time found her severed head beside a spring and decided to fit it back into place. Having got it fixed neatly into the correct position her life became miraculously restored and she lived out the rest of it in such a saintly way that she received official recognition. Moreover, the spring beside which the miracle was performed, (if you can find it) is said to possess healing powers. According to old guidebooks there are petrified springs all around the area.

Branscombe

HANGMAN'S STONE (north of Branscombe on the A3052)

A man, having stolen a sheep paused in his exertions to rest against this stone while he recovered his breath. Whereupon the sheep, alarmed at the situation, jumped frantically about on the end of the imprisoning rope, dealt him rougher justice than he really deserved by entangling the rope around his neck and strangling him.

LACE MAKING

Lace making is traditionally one of the staple industries of Branscombe, and women worked away at their ancient craft at the doorways of their thatched cottages. Mr. Tucker, who lived in the village was one of the principal lace merchants in the county, employing several hundred people. In 1851, spendid local lacework, valued at £3,000 was exhibited at the Crystal Palace in London.

THE COAST
THE LANDSLIP OF 1790

The Underhooken was the descriptive local name for the undercliff caused by the landslide of 1790, since when the wild, luxuriant growth which has colonised has created an area of striking beauty and an invaluable habitat of great scientific interest. The landslip, similar in many ways to that at Bindon in 1839, also forced up a reef offshore. It was recorded that places on which the fishermen had laid their crabpots 8 to 11 feet beneath the water, and which they had sailed across the previous night had suddenly reared far above sea level. They were astonished next morning to find their pots poised on a reef jutting 15 feet or so into the air. Nearly 10 acres of land had dropped 200 to 260 feet, vertically, like a straight slab of cake, moved seawards, becoming broken up forming columns and pinnacles.

THE CLIFFS

Thus Hooken Cliff was one of the first landslips of the Devon and Dorset coast. The coastline is lofty, imposing and extremely beautiful with rocks festooned with ivy and creepers providing a wonderful habitat for the wildlife. The cliffs rise to over 400 feet on the east and over 500 feet to the west.

VIEWS AND INSPIRATION

There are magnificent views from the hilltops across the orchards and cornfields on the hillsides and taking in a seascape of subtle contrasts. Visiting the 'dear, queer funny old place' earlier this century W. H. Hudson found everything he needed to restore his spirits; 'The wildness and freedom of untilled earth; the unobstructed prospect, hills beyond hills of malachite, stretching away along the coast into infinitude, long leagues of red sea wall and the wide expanse and everlasting freshness of ocean.' It similarly caught the imagination of the writer H. J. Massingham and has been a magnet for other writers and artists. Gulls, nesting on the cliff ledges and other sea birds also appreciate some of these finer points and noble birds of prey (now less common) traditionally colonised the area.

Ye Olde Mason's Arms, Branscombe

TRACES OF PRE-HISTORY

The headlands and surrounding areas bear traces of pre-history and on Berry Cliff, west of Branscombe Mouth is a large, rectangular earthwork of unknown age and beyond it are a number of barrows. There is evidence of Neolithic flint workings where the ground has been left with hummocks and terraces. An old guidebook stated that near the summit of Dunscombe Cliff there was 'a layer of shells, which have been converted into calcedony, and a bed of rolled chalk flints.' An opening half way up the cliffs is the remains of an early quarry.

There is evidence of Roman occupation; a coin of Victorinus, dating from about A.D. 261 was found on the hill above Berry Barton and a Roman brooch was discovered on a site lower down.

FISHERMEN AND FARMERS

The unprotected nature of the shore at Branscombe made fishing impractical at times during the year and this gave rise to the tradition of fishermen having smallholdings on the steep, sheltered, cliffside slopes as a back-up means of livelihood. They did particularly well with their early potatoes.

WALKING

The area is a delight for walkers and the South West Peninsula Coastal Path runs to the east and to the west. A footpath leads from near the Mason's Arms to the shore and links with the coastal paths.

TEA ROOMS

The unusual thatched tea rooms at Branscombe Mouth was formerly a part of the store place for the coal imported from Wales by sea to fuel the lime kilns on the cliffs. The building, which became derelict for many years is now transformed and provides a welcome service for visitors.

THE VILLAGE TODAY

The villagers are proud of their heritage and pursue a way of life at a comfortable distance from the general 'rat race'. Having escaped vulgar development which has devalued some other coastal parts, Branscombe remains one of the most natural, charming and attractive places on the south coast.

* * * * *

THE GEOLOGY OF THE COASTLINE WEST OF AXMOUTH

The landscape of the Seaton district is a plateau, consisting of Cretaceous rocks (Chalk, Upper Greensand) capped by flinty gravel deposits, entrenched by the deep valleys of the Axe river, its tributaries and the streams at Branscombe. The plateau is generally about 500 feet (150 metres) above sea level and it ends to the seaward in high cliffs.

In general, the rock formations along the cliffs of the south coast of England become progressively older from east to west — from the Tertiary sands and clays of Bournemouth Bay through the Cretaceous rocks of East Dorset, the Jurassic rocks of West Dorset, the red Permo-Trias of East Devon, and the older, Palaeozoic rocks of South Devon and Cornwall. Between Lyme Regis and Seaton the coastal slopes consist of landslips in Jurassic rocks (mainly the Lias, layers of blue clay and limestone) beneath the Chalk and Upper Greensand capping. At Seaton the red rocks of East Devon appear in the cliffs; they are visible on the western side of Seaton Bay, and especially between Branscombe and Sidmouth. These red Permian and Triassic rocks are mainly clays and marls, with some sandstone, and some conglomerates which consist of layers of gravel deposited in ancient desert wadis. (The best example of these is seen just to the west of Budleigh Salterton.)

Beer Head consists of Chalk cliffs, with tumbled boulders below and to the west is Hooken Landslip. The coast at Hooken consisted of sheer Chalk cliffs in the middle of the 18th century, but during the winter of 1789/90 a deep fissure appeared behind the cliff crest, and in March 1790 the landslip occurred, the Chalk and Upper Greensand collapsing seawards over the soft underlying Triassic clays. The result was a tumbled undercliff, with columns and pinnacles of Chalk and Greensand separated by clefts and chasms; a rugged topography which quickly became overgrown with scrub and woodland creating the densely vegetated area that we see today, and a valuable habitat for the wildlife.

The River Axe has incised a wide, deep valley into the coastal plateau. During the later stages of the Pleistocene ice age — about 20,000 years ago — the Axe drained down to a much lower sea level, and cut out a still deeper valley downstream from Musbury. Then, as the world's climate became warmer, much of the Pleistocene ice melted, water flowed back into the oceans, and sea level rose, flooding back into the broad lowland of the English Channel, and submerging the lower reaches of valleys such as the Axe. The rising sea also brought waves to attack the coastline, cutting cliffs, triggering landslips, and deriving beaches of flint and chert gravel, which now line much of the coast between Sidmouth and Branscombe, and also occupy the shores of Beer Cove and Seaton Bay. Drifting from west to east, in response to waves generated by the prevailing south westerly winds, this shingle built up across the mouth of the marine inlet. Subsequently, silt and clay washed down the river has accumulated in marshlands, which now border the shrunken muddy estuary, carrying salt marsh vegetation, reeds and rushes. The estuary remains a tidal channel, flooded twice daily as the tide rises, and draining out during the ebb when mudflats are exposed. The mouth of the Axe, deflected eastwards by drifting shingle, has been partly stabilised by the building of a breakwater on the eastern shore, but it remains difficult to navigate. A shingle bar, variable in form and dimensions, is usually present just off the river mouth. This is shingle by-passing the outlet, and moving on eastwards.

The Branscombe stream, much smaller than the Axe, has nevertheless cut out a deep valley in the coastal plateau, its tributaries draining branching valleys which head back near the main road (A3052). The shingle beach is wide and high here, and the stream outflow percolates through it to the sea.

The cove at Beer has been cut back by the sea at the mouth of a small valley incised into the Chalk. The cliffs here show layers of flint nodules which are released by weathering and erosion, then rolled and rounded by wave scour to form the blue cobbles that dominate the beach. Inland, Beer Stone, a form of hard chalk is quarried and has been used in many fine buildings locally and far away.

West of Branscombe the coast is very steep, with a capping of Upper Greensand and flint gravel, and slumping slopes of red Triassic marl. In places, fallen masses of Greensand form bouldery 'ebbs', so called because they run out to sea and are exposed at low tide.

*　*　*　*　*